Ripley's Believe It or Not!®

Developed and produced by Ripley Publishing Ltd

This edition published and distributed by:

Mason Crest
450 Parkway Drive, Suite D, Broomall, PA 19008
www.masoncrest.com

Printed and bound in the United States of America

First printing
9 8 7 6 5 4 3 2 1

Ripley's Believe It or Not!
Crazy Animals
ISBN: 978-1-4222-3149-4 (hardback)
Ripley's Believe It or Not!—Complete 8 Title Series
ISBN: 978-1-4222-3147-0

Cataloging-in-Publication Data is on file with the Library of Congress

PUBLISHER'S NOTE
While every effort has been made to verify the accuracy of the entries in this book, the
Publishers cannot be held responsible for any errors contained in the work. They would
be glad to receive any information from readers.

WARNING
Some of the stunts and activities in this book are undertaken by experts and should not
be attempted by anyone without adequate training and supervision.

Ripley's Believe It or Not!

Download The Weird

CRAZY ANIMALS

www.MasonCrest.com

CRAZY ANIMALS

Open up to find some incredible creatures. Meet the dog that can ride a scooter, the horse with a mustache, and the largest crocodile ever!

Brutus, a two-ton saltwater crocodile that lives in Australia, measures 18 ft (5 m) long and has only one arm...

Despite being born with two faces, two mouths, two noses, and three eyes, Frank and Louie, a cat owned by Marty Stevens of Worcester, Massachusetts, has set a world record by living to the age of 12. Most Janus cats——named after a Roman god with two faces——fail to survive, often because their two mouths cause them to choke. However, although both of Frank and Louie's noses work, only one mouth does. The nonfunctioning mouth isn't connected to his sole esophagus, meaning that he can't eat with it. Frank and Louie has a single brain, meaning both faces react simultaneously.

TWO-FACED CAT

HAPPY SNAPPERS

Brutus, an 18-ft-long (5.5-m), two-ton saltwater crocodile on the Adelaide River in Australia's Northern Territory, has a fearsome reputation. The 80-year-old monster, who can be lured out of the water by dangling kangaroo meat from a pole to allow riverboat tourists to take frightening close-up photos, has such powerful jaws that he once bit a log cutter's noisy chainsaw in half... while the log cutter hid up a tree. Brutus is not invincible, however, having lost his right front leg during a fight with a shark in the river estuary.

Missing arm!

CONFUSED CAT Overcoming her natural tendencies, a female cat named Niu Niu acted as a mother to 30 newborn chicks. Her owner, farmer Lao Yang of Suibin County, China, was amazed to see the cat licking, embracing, and playing with the chicks, who responded by following her everywhere.

AIRPLANES IN THE UNITED STATES COLLIDE WITH AN AVERAGE OF ONE ALLIGATOR A YEAR ON RUNWAYS.

BEST FRIENDS A mynah bird and a dog have become so inseparable that their owner has built a special perch for the bird that can be attached to the dog and enables them to go for walks together. Qiao Yu of Shandong Province, China, says the mynah combs the dog's fur and plucks fleas off it, while the dog responds by barking loudly whenever someone goes near the bird.

POOPED PARK A campground in Cornwall, England, faced a $15,000 clean-up bill in February 2011 after a huge flock comprising tens of thousands of starlings covered it in a layer of bird droppings that was 7 in (18 cm) deep in places.

BEST BUDDIES
In a real-life version of Timon and Simba from the movie *The Lion King*, Marcell Tournier's pet meerkat Bob cuddles up to Zinzi the lion cub at his home in Sun City, South Africa. Zinzi was rescued by safari-park owner Marcell after being abandoned by her mother, and she and Bob have since become inseparable.

UNINVITED GUEST After floodwaters receded from her home in Parauapebas, Brazil, in February 2011, a woman was shocked to find an alligator behind the couch in the living room—and her three-year-old son happily patting the 5-ft-long (1.5-m) reptile on the head.

LONG CAT Stewie, a five-year-old Maine Coon cat owned by Robin Hendrickson and Erik Brandsness of Reno, Nevada, measures more than 4 ft (1.2 m) long from the tip of his nose to the tip of his tail.

TRACTOR LOVE For more than three years, a swan in the grounds of a luxury hotel in Velen, Germany, has been madly in love with a big blue tractor and follows the vehicle around wherever it goes. The swan—named Schwani—also finds diggers and machines on the building site next door interesting. Animal behaviorists believe the bird probably had contact with machines as a cygnet and therefore sees the tractor as a likely mate.

Rainbow Chicks

Chickens are dyed with artificial coloring to make them more appealing to buyers at a market in Semarang, Central Java, Indonesia.

PANDA SUITS

To prepare captive-born giant panda cubs for life in the wild, keepers at the panda conservation centers in western China dress up in fluffy black-and-white panda costumes. They wear the suits whenever approaching the cubs so that the pandas have only minimum contact with humans. Here, baby panda Tao Tao is being transferred to a large wilderness area where it is planned he and his captive-bred mother, Cao Cao, will start their reintegration into the wild.

🅡 SKINNY SCAVENGERS Hagfish are primitive, tubelike scavengers that eat using their skin. On finding a carcass on the ocean floor, the hagfish burrows into the dead body, where it not only uses its mouth to eat, but also absorbs nutrients through its skin and gills.

🅡 BLIND SHEEPDOG Liz Edwards, a farmer in Cheshire, England, bought Jack, a sheepdog that was so good at his job it took several months for her to realize the dog had gone blind. "He's such an inspiration," she said. "He carried on as if nothing had happened. He must have had our farm mapped out in his head. He knows exactly where everything is." She discovered he had lost vision in both eyes only when he ran straight into a wooden peg sticking out of the ground.

🅡 MUCUS COCOON Some species of parrotfish spend up to an hour each night preparing a cocoon of mucus, which they wrap around themselves like a sleeping bag.

🅡 DOLPHIN SCAN Tapeko, a female bottlenose dolphin, had her pregnancy confirmed by undergoing a human-style ultrasound scan at Brookfield Zoo, Illinois. The dolphin was happy to float belly-up for the scan—in return for a fish reward.

🅡 NATURAL PRAWN KILLERS The Mantis shrimp of the Indian and Pacific oceans has a sting as powerful as a shot from a .22-caliber bullet. They kill prey by dismembering or spearing it with their claws, but can also stun it with their fearsome sting.

🅡 SAVIOR LILLY After suffering a bad epileptic fit, Nathan Cooper of Bournemouth, England, came close to death—but was saved by his cat Lilly, who alerted Nathan's parents. She can detect the weekly fits her owner experiences before they happen, and once resuscitated him by licking his mouth. Experts think cats' and dogs' acute sense of smell helps them detect minute chemical changes within the human body prior to a fit.

🅡 JURY SERVICE Tabby Sal the cat was summoned to do jury service in Boston, Massachusetts, even after his owner Anna Esposito told the court he was "unable to speak and understand English" and was "a domestic short-haired neutered feline."

THE LARGEST JELLYFISH EVER CAUGHT HAD TENTACLES 120 FT (36 M) LONG!

🅡 GATOR DRAG Ten-year-old Michael Dasher of Rockledge, Florida, dragged a live alligator, measuring 5 ft 9 in (1.75 m) in length, home from a nearby canal. The boy was fishing with friends when the alligator snapped at the line and ran at him. He hit it with sticks and jumped on its back before dragging it home, suffering just minor scratches on his arms and hands.

Giant Croc

A huge saltwater crocodile weighing more than a ton is thought to be the largest specimen ever captured. The 21-ft-long (6.4-m) monster weighed 2,370 lb (1,075 kg), that's well over a ton, and had been hunted by villagers in the Philippines for nearly a month following a spate of attacks on humans and animals. It may have eaten a farmer who went missing in July 2011, along with several water buffaloes near the town of Bunawan, where the head of a 12-year-old girl was also bitten off by a crocodile in 2009. The record-breaking croc was so big that it took 30 local men to capture it, and it could fit three men inside it at once. Sadly, the croc died at an ecotourism park in 2013.

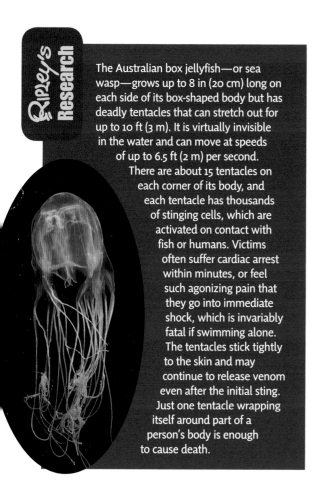

The Australian box jellyfish—or sea wasp—grows up to 8 in (20 cm) long on each side of its box-shaped body but has deadly tentacles that can stretch out for up to 10 ft (3 m). It is virtually invisible in the water and can move at speeds of up to 6.5 ft (2 m) per second. There are about 15 tentacles on each corner of its body, and each tentacle has thousands of stinging cells, which are activated on contact with fish or humans. Victims often suffer cardiac arrest within minutes, or feel such agonizing pain that they go into immediate shock, which is invariably fatal if swimming alone. The tentacles stick tightly to the skin and may continue to release venom even after the initial sting. Just one tentacle wrapping itself around part of a person's body is enough to cause death.

Jellyfish Survivor

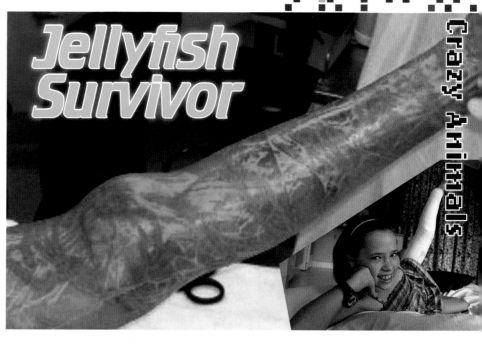

Ten-year-old Rachael Shardlow is the first person known to have survived an extensive sting from a box jellyfish—one of the world's most venomous creatures. She was stung while swimming in the Calliope River, Queensland, Australia, and after her brother pulled her from the water, she fell unconscious with the jellyfish's lethal tentacles still strapped to her limbs. Rachael required six weeks of hospital treatment before being allowed home.

⑧ SECRET DRINKER After checking the plumbing of hot tubs that appeared to have been leaking water, workers at the Etali Safari Lodge in North West Province, South Africa, discovered the culprit wasn't in fact a water leak—but actually a thirsty elephant. They nicknamed the elephant "Troublesome."

⑧ LONG-DISTANCE SWIM A migrating humpback whale swam 6,200 mi (10,000 km) from Brazil to Madagascar—a quarter of the way around the world. She was spotted off the coast of Brazil in 1999 and just over two years later, identified by the distinctive markings on her tail, she was seen in the Indian Ocean off the east coast of Madagascar.

⑧ SELF-SUFFICIENT The spiny-shelled species of deep-sea snail, *Alviniconcha hessleri*, lives near geothermal vents and gets its food from bacteria that live within its own gills.

⑧ SNAKE ISLAND Although Shedao Island, China, covers only 180 acres (73 ha), it is home to over 15,000 poisonous pit vipers.

Gargantua the Great

Gargantua the Great was billed as "the world's most terrifying living creature" and was described by noted journalist Heywood Broun as "the fiercest looking thing I have ever seen on two legs." An African lowland gorilla, he was said to be the largest gorilla ever exhibited, weighing some 600 lb (272 kg)—a whopping 160 lb (72 kg) heavier than the average lowland gorilla.

Gargantua was captured as a baby in the Belgian Congo in the late 1920s and given to a sea captain as a pet. He traveled with the captain and was popular with the crew until a drunken sailor threw acid in his face on the voyage from Africa to the United States The attack left him with a scarred face and increasingly aggressive behavior.

Unable to cope with him, the captain presented the young gorilla to eccentric animal lover Gertrude Lintz who cared for sick creatures in Brooklyn, New York. She named him Buddy and nursed him back to health, including chewing his food for him, and even arranging

for plastic surgery on his scar, leaving him with a permanent sneer. She used to drive around Brooklyn with the gorilla, dressed in clothes, in the passenger seat. However, one night a thunderstorm panicked Buddy, who smashed his way out of his cage and went looking for his "mother" for comfort. By then he weighed about 460 lb (209 kg), so Mrs. Lintz sold him to the Ringling Bros. and Barnum & Bailey

Circus for $10,000 in 1938. At the circus, Buddy was renamed Gargantua the Great on account of his size and mean disposition and went on to become its star attraction. Visitors were not allowed to go near his cage because, with a reach of 5 ft (1.5 m), he could grab people to whom he took a dislike. The most feared ape in the Western world, Gargantua died of pneumonia in 1949.

Gargantua the Gorilla, with his trademark sneer, which was the result of plastic surgery to repair acid-burn scars on his face.

A circus poster advertising the spectacle of the enormous gorilla

Gargantua was fed a host of medicines to keep him healthy during winter

TWO-HEADED SNAKE

Beating odds of more than 10,000 to one, a two-headed albino Honduran milk snake was hatched by a Florida conservation group. A few days later, the snake's right head ate its first meal—a small mouse—while the left head watched.

X-ray showing where the snake's spines are fused together

CAPTIVE ANIMAL STARS

Jumbo the elephant

Standing 11 ft 6 in (3.5 m) tall and weighing 6.5 tons, Jumbo was the star attraction at England's London Zoo for 17 years. He was sold in 1882 to the Barnum & Bailey Circus in the United States for $10,000, prompting outrage from the British public. He died three years later, hit by a train while trying to lead a younger elephant to safety.

Chi Chi the giant panda

When she arrived at London Zoo from China in 1958, Chi Chi was the only giant panda in the Western world and a source of great curiosity. She inspired the World Wildlife Fund logo, but repeated attempts to get her to mate with Moscow Zoo's giant panda, An An, failed.

Clarence the cross-eyed lion

TV producer Ivan Tors discovered Clarence, a cross-eyed lion, at "Africa U.S.A.," a wildlife park in Soledad Canyon, California. The gentle beast went on to star in his own 1965 movie Clarence the Cross-Eyed Lion and the TV series Daktari.

Congo the chimpanzee

A chimpanzee at London Zoo from 1954 to 1964, Congo was a talented artist and had completed 400 paintings by the age of four. Pablo Picasso was a fan of Congo's work and hung one of the chimp's paintings on his studio wall.

Bart the Kodiak bear

Trained in Utah by Doug and Lynne Seus, Bart was a male Alaskan Kodiak bear, standing 9 ft 6 in (2.9 m) tall and weighing 1,500 lb (680 kg), who appeared in several movies—opposite the likes of Brad Pitt, Alec Baldwin, and Anthony Hopkins. Bart died in 2000 at age 23 while filming the documentary Growing Up Grizzly.

NEW EYES When seeing-eye dog Edward lost his eyesight, he got his own seeing-eye dog! Edward the Labrador had helped partially sighted Graham Waspe of Suffolk, England, for six years but then suffered glaucoma and had to have both eyes removed. So another dog, two-year-old Opal, joined the family and now helps both Graham and Edward to get around.

CHATTY CHIMP Kanzi, a mature bonobo ape, has a vocabulary of around 450 words, up to 40 of which he uses daily. Dr. Sue Savage-Rumbaugh of Des Moines, Iowa, has taught Kanzi to "speak" by pointing at different symbols on a computer.

FOUR-FOOTED DUCK A duck born in China's Guangxi Province had three legs and four feet. Behind its normal two legs, the duckling had a third leg with two feet, probably the result of a genetic mutation.

RAIN ALLERGY Researchers in the remote mountain forests of Burma have discovered a species of snub-nosed monkey that sneezes whenever it rains. To avoid getting rainwater in its upturned nose, the monkey spends wet days sitting with its head between its knees.

TITANIUM TEETH Axel, a prison guard dog from Melbourne, Australia, was fitted with titanium teeth after losing his real ones when they shattered as he bit into a bed board.

MINI MARVEL Weighing just 2½ lb (1.1 kg), Nancy the Chihuahua has a natural talent for herding sheep several times her size. Owner Ali Taylor says that Britain's tiniest sheep dog learned her trade from watching border collies in action.

HIGH LIFE During construction of the Shard skyscraper in London, England, a fox was found living on the 72nd floor—944 ft (290 m) above the ground. The animal entered the building through a central stairwell before climbing to the top, where for over two weeks it lived on scraps left behind by builders.

BIG MOUTH Owing to its loosely hinged mouth, a gulper eel can swallow prey with a volume ten times the size of its own body.

SMOKING CHIMP A chimpanzee that became addicted to smoking cigarettes died in 2010 at age 52—ten years longer than the life expectancy of an average chimp. Charlie the Smoking Chimp picked up the unhealthy habit from visitors to Manguang Zoo, near Bloemfontein, South Africa, who threw him lit cigarettes through the bars of his enclosure.

RABBIT HEATING Up to 6,000 nuisance rabbits in Stockholm, Sweden, are culled each year and taken to an incinerator in Karlskoga where their carcasses are burned and processed for biofuel to heat nearby homes.

Pugs Might Fly

On August 15, 2011, in the skies above California, Otis the skydiving pug made his 64th jump with his master, veteran skydiver Will DaSilva. Otis has been skydiving in a special tandem harness with his owner for more than nine years and seems to love every minute of the ride.

CAT IN A VAT

Ksyusha, a white-haired Himalayan kitten, can somehow squeeze herself into a small glass jar. Her owner, Yuriy Korotun of Moscow, Russia, says the kitten—nicknamed "Mewdini"—loves to curl up in confined spaces but always manages to escape unharmed.

DIVING GEAR Gannets dive headfirst into the sea at speeds of up to 90 mph (145 km/h) and can reach depths of 30 ft (9 m) below the water surface. To withstand the impact as they hit the water, the birds have an extra-thick skull that acts as a crash helmet, as well as a throat pouch that inflates like a little airbag to protect their body during the plunge.

WORKING MONKEYS Two baby monkeys, Nehime and Rakan, work as station masters at Hojomachi station on the Hojo railway line in Japan's Hyogo Prefecture in an attempt to boost visitors to the rail line. The monkeys wear special blue uniforms and miniature hats.

NATURAL DAREDEVILS To avoid predators, barnacle geese build nests high on mountain cliffs—and at just three days old, the tiny goslings must jump from nests as far up as 300 ft (90 m) to reach food on the ground.

KEEP AWAY Mandrill monkeys have leaned how to perform sign language to tell other group members to keep away. They place one hand loosely over their eyes, but with their fingers parted slightly so that they can still see. While the hand is in place, the other mandrills at Colchester Zoo, England, keep their distance.

CLEAN SWEEP A golden retriever uses a specially made small broom to sweep the streets of Changchun, Jilin Province, China, while walking with his owner Xu Ming. The dog takes the broom everywhere and, under Xu's instructions, runs in a zigzag pattern to sweep away dust and debris.

TAIL FORCE
Thresher sharks have a tail that can grow as long as the rest of their body. They use it to smack and stun their prey.

DOUBLE TROUBLE
Oscar the Labrador and his 53-year-old master both survived with just broken bones after plunging 200 ft (60 m) over the edge of a cliff in North Yorkshire, England. After Oscar fell off the cliff, his owner was desperately trying to work out how to reach his pet when a strong gust of wind blew him over the edge, too.

DANGEROUS DANCE As part of their courtship ritual, pairs of bald eagles perform a cartwheel dance, soaring high into the air, locking their talons together, then spinning out of control toward the ground, breaking off at the very last second to fly upward again.

VERSATILE SWIMMER The black ghost knifefish, found in the rivers of South America, is able to swim forward or backward equally well and navigates by emitting a small electric charge.

MAIL MISERY Toby, a Jack Russell terrier belonging to Gill Bird of Hampshire, England, chewed up his owner's mail—and the combination of the envelope glue and wet paper glued his mouth shut.

FISH OUT OF WATER A 1-ft-long (30-cm) sturgeon dropped at night from the sky (probably by a heron) on a lawn in Worcester, England, was found the next morning, having survived thanks to the moisture on the grass.

DANCING DOLPHINS Wild dolphins are teaching themselves to "walk" using their tails on the ocean surface. Researchers in Australia say dolphins have developed the art of tail-walking, which seems to have no practical use and has been compared to dancing in humans.

GATOR SNATCH After a 6-ft-long (1.8-m) alligator snatched his Jack Russell terrier Lizabeth while walking along the Hillsborough River in Tampa, Florida, Tom Martino fired shots into the water to force the reptile to release the dog. He then performed CPR on Lizabeth until she started breathing again.

TOMBSTONING MONKEYS

Mimicking the human tombstoning craze of jumping from great heights into water, these thrill-seeking macaques in Jaipur, India, climb a 12-ft-high (3.6-m) lamppost and then hurl themselves into a shallow trough of water—apparently just for fun. Even a ring of barbed wire around the lamppost could not stop their crazy antics. Macaques have also been seen jumping from 9-ft (2.7-m) rocks into the sea off Thailand and are one of the few primates that are not scared of water.

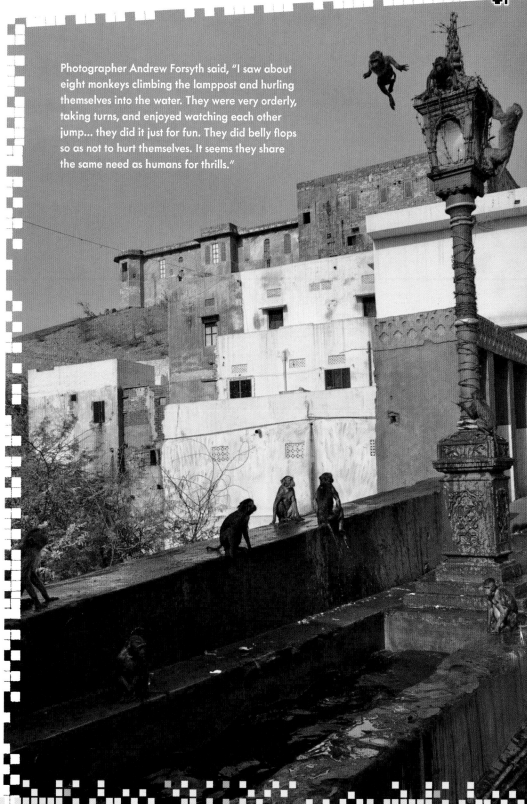

Photographer Andrew Forsyth said, "I saw about eight monkeys climbing the lamppost and hurling themselves into the water. They were very orderly, taking turns, and enjoyed watching each other jump... they did it just for fun. They did belly flops so as not to hurt themselves. It seems they share the same need as humans for thrills."

HAIRY HORSE

Alfie, a black shire-horse cross from Bristol, England, has a 7-in-long (18-cm) blond mustache. While most horses with mustaches have them trimmed every six months, Alfie's has been growing for more than five years because he refuses to let the stable hands get close enough to shave it off.

SWEET REVENGE Oystercatcher birds have bladelike beaks for prying open shellfish—but sometimes their prey does get the better of them, holding their beaks in place until the birds drown.

SHORT LEGS The Munchkin breed of cats has a mutation that gives it short legs and a stature similar to dachshund or corgi dogs. Although short-legged cats were known in the early 20th century, the breed was not rediscovered until 1983 when Louisiana music teacher Sandra Hochenedel found two pregnant cats. Half of the kittens in one litter were short-legged, and today's Munchkin cats are descended from that line.

BIRD RESCUE When his pet dog carried a limp goose that had been hit by a car into the yard of his home in Urumchi, China, Yu Yanping thought the dog would eat it. Instead, the dog licked the bird until it recovered, and the two went on to become inseparable, feeding from the same bowl and even sharing the dog's kennel.

STOWAWAY KITTEN Amy Bindman of Calgary, Canada, found a kitten in a shipping container sent from China. It had survived being sealed away without food or water for nearly 45 days.

ROBBERS ATTACKED Two armed robbers who held up a tobacco store in Altadena, California, fled after being attacked by the owner's pet Chihuahua. Little Paco refused to be intimidated even when one of the robbers pointed a shotgun at him, and chased the men out of the shop and down the street.

HORSE FALL A horse stumbled through an open window and landed in the basement of her owners' home in Elbert County, Colorado. It took rescue teams four hours to get the mare—named Summer—out of the house.

SPEEDING HORSE A police roadside camera designed to catch speeding drivers in Meppen, Germany, caught something different on film in July 2011—a runaway horse. The horse had escaped from a paddock and galloped off down a busy main road into the town. The speeding driver who triggered the picture pleaded to be excused the automatic fine because he claimed he was simply trying to get away from the horse.

VULTURE ARRESTED Finding a griffon vulture in Hyaal, Saudi Arabia, carrying a GPS transmitter and a tag from Tel Aviv University, Saudi security services held the bird in custody on suspicion of spying for the Israeli intelligence agency Mossad. However, wildlife experts pointed out that the vulture was simply part of a migration study and the bird was eventually released without charge.

COLD COMFORT When the Arctic ground squirrel goes into hibernation during long Arctic winters, its body temperature drops below the freezing point of water to 26.4°F (−3°C). Scientists have yet to discover another mammal that survives with such a low body temperature.

HOUND HOTEL Alongside its normal rooms for human guests, the Riverside Hotel in Evesham, England, has three dog suites that provide luxury accommodation for pets. Dogs staying there can feast from a special canine menu, swim in a spa pool, and have their portrait done.

CONSTANT COMPANIONS Jane Hartley of Loughborough, England, loves her pet parrots Fiz and Buzz so much that she takes them shopping, cycling, walking, and even skiing. The small birds sit on her hand while she cycles, and nestle in her pocket as she hurtles down Alpine mountains during skiing vacations.

OCTOPUS SPRAY A common octopus at an aquarium in England has been called Squirt because he deliberately aims a jet of water at visitors. The inquisitive octopus learned to lift the top part of his body above the water in his tank so that he could look around and then realized that if he breathed out while he was doing it, he could fire a stream of water like a hose. Octopuses draw water into their body to absorb the oxygen from it and then pass it out again through special tubes alongside their beak.

R ROTTEN LOOK *Nimbochromis livingstonii*, a fish found in Africa's Lake Malawi, has the blotchy appearance of a rotting fish and lies motionless on the lakebed to attract the scavengers on which it preys.

R SPIN CYCLE An eight-week-old kitten named Princess survived an hour-long spin in a washing machine after creeping unnoticed into the drum. It was only when her owner, Susan Gordon of Aberdeen, Scotland, was removing the clean items from the machine that she spotted the sodden kitten.

R BUNNY CART The O'Rourke family of Tucson, Arizona, discovered an abandoned baby rabbit in their garden that could not use his hind legs. They built a little cart on wheels and strapped it to the rabbit's rear so that he no longer had to drag his legs behind him.

R HOURGLASS FIGURE Debbie Pearson of New Orleans, Louisiana, cares for a turtle that grew with a plastic ring from a milk jug around the middle of its shell. When it was a tiny hatchling, it crawled into the ring which proceeded to grow around it so that its shell now resembles a figure eight.

R RESCUE CENTER Ha Wenjin gave up her job and sold her house, car, and jewelry to adopt more than 1,500 stray dogs at her rescue center in Nanjing, China. She employs 12 people to care for the dogs and to look after 200 adopted cats at a second center nearby.

SLEEPY BIRD

After eating a hearty meal of ants, a green woodpecker appears to have been caught dozing against the branch of this tree in Worcestershire, England.

TO KEEP FROM DRIFTING AWAY FROM EACH OTHER, SEA OTTERS HOLD PAWS WHILE THEY SLEEP.

R WIDE WINGS Queen Alexandra's Birdwing—a butterfly found only in Papua New Guinea—can grow to have a 1-ft-long (30-cm) wingspan.

R BODY HEAT Sea otters lack blubber to insulate themselves, so they must eat up to one-quarter of their body weight every day in order to generate enough heat to keep warm.

One beady eye!

CYCLOPS SHARK

A fisherman in Mexico landed what might well be a one of a kind—an albino baby shark with just one eye, located centrally above the mouth. He actually caught the mother, a 286-lb (130-kg) bull shark, but when she was filleted, ten pups were found inside, including her Cyclops offspring.

TATTOOED FISH

Tattooed goldfish are sold at a pet market in Changchun, China, for around $12 each. Laser-inscribed decorations on the fish include flowery patterns and the Chinese characters for sentiments such as "wealth," "longevity," and "happiness." Personalized messages are also available.

WEALTH

HAPPINESS

KEYCHAIN CREATURES

Live fish, tiny tortoises, and young giant salamanders, all sealed in plastic pouches, are sold as keychains at a roadside stall in Beijing, China. The vendor says that a special liquid inside the pouches provides all the necessary oxygen and nutrients for the creatures.

HIDDEN MENACE People swam about in a public pool in Darwin, Australia, unaware that a 20-in (50-cm) baby saltwater crocodile was lurking in the deep end. The reptile, which was thought to be a rubber toy until it tried to bite a handler, was rescued and released back into the wild.

REINDEER REFLECTIONS In an attempt to reduce the number of car crashes that kill around 500 reindeer each year in Norway, 2,000 of the animals were fitted with reflective yellow collars or small antler tags, making them more visible in the dark.

FISHY TALE Two goldfish survived 134 days without food or electricity to power their tank filter following the 2011 earthquake in Christchurch, New Zealand. Shaggy and Daphne—named after *Scooby Doo* characters—spent over four months left unattended in an accountants' reception area, but pulled through by eating algae growing on the side of the tank.

DRUNKEN OWL A brown owl was spotted sitting by the side of a busy road in Pforzheim, Germany, seemingly oblivious to passing traffic. The feathery friend did not appear to be injured, but one of its eyelids was drooping noticeably. Looking around, police found two empty bottles of Schnapps nearby and realized that in fact the bird was drunk. So the police took the owl into custody and gave it plenty of water until it sobered up.

SHAGGY DOG STORY

Norman, a shaggy Briard dog owned by the Cobb family of Canton, Georgia, has been riding a scooter since he was a puppy. He balances on the scooter unaided with his front paws resting over the handlebars while he pushes himself along using his hind leg. Videos of his tricks have been a massive hit on YouTube, and he even has his own Facebook page.

LONG TAIL

A calf born on Jennifer Showalter's farm in Fairfield, Virginia, on September 15, 2011, had a tail that was 60 in (1.5 m) long! Calves' tails are usually between just 5 and 8 in (13 and 20 cm) long.

TWO-HEADED TORTOISE Magdalena, a tortoise owned by Roman Gresak from Zilina, Slovakia, has two heads and five legs. Each of the heads has its own nerve system and the tortoise has two brains, which work independently of each other, meaning that sometimes the second head wants to go in a different direction to the first!

COLOR CHANGE *Rhacophorus penanorum*, a species of tiny frog that lives on the island of Borneo, has bright green skin at night but changes color to brown by day—and its eyes match it by changing color, too.

FIVE EARS A cat named Luntya, found wandering the streets of Voronezh, Russia, has five ears. She has two normal ears, two extra ears turned at an angle of 180 degrees, and a tiny fifth ear.

SMALL COW Swallow, an 11-year-old cow owned by Caroline Ryder of West Yorkshire, England, stands only 33 in (84 cm) tall at the shoulder, making her shorter than most sheep.

ORANGE FLOCK After losing 200 of his sheep to rustlers, farmer John Heard from Devon, England, took drastic action—he painted his entire flock orange. The harmless dip of orange dye made the sheep so visible that thieves left them alone.

ESCAPED CROC A 6-ft-long (1.8-m) crocodile that was taken by a photographer to Lake Shira, Siberia, to pose for pictures with tourists caused panic when it escaped into the water, terrifying hundreds of swimmers. The reptile bolted for freedom while the photographer was haggling with tourists over the price of a souvenir photo.

COW BEDS Dairy farmers in Norway are required by law to provide a place for their cows to lie down—such as rubber mattresses.

MIXED LITTER A female Dalmatian dog in Meridiano, Brazil, adopted a piglet and a baby goat and allowed them to suckle her alongside her puppies. The puppies accepted the newcomers, both of which were also black and white.

COPYCAT SQUIRREL Jim Watkins of Carthage, Mississippi, rescued a stranded baby squirrel that his pet cat and her kittens then adopted. The squirrel soon learned how to purr for affection like a cat.

ALBINO ACTORS Showbiz manager Tom Beser has set up the world's first acting agency for albino animals. From his base in Rheinfelden, Germany, he leases his collection of albino creatures—including lizards, minks, and a raccoon—to moviemakers for films and TV commercials.

CRACKING CROWS Crows in Japan have been seen placing walnuts on roads, waiting for cars to drive over them to crack open the shells, and then flying back to feast on the nuts' contents.

ANCIENT TORTOISE Jonathan, a giant tortoise on the South Atlantic island of St. Helena, is at least 178 years old. His life has spanned eight British monarchs and 37 U.S. presidents, yet he still has the energy to mate with three younger females. The St. Helena five-pence coin has a picture of Jonathan on its reverse.

MIMICKING MOM A keeper at China's Wuhan Zoo has to wear a black-and-white-striped T-shirt every day to persuade a newborn, orphaned zebra that he is its mother. Chen Nong realized that whenever he wore black and white the baby zebra became excited, and soon it would take milk from him only if he wore that zebralike shirt.

HORSE ARTIST A nine-year-old, 1,500-lb (681-kg) Friesian horse named Justin has produced a series of paintings, which have been exhibited in art galleries and have sold for hundreds of dollars. His owner, Adonna Combs of Columbus, Indiana, first spotted his talent when he used her whip to draw patterns in the sand. Encouraged with carrots—he goes through 5 lb (2.2 kg) per painting—he holds the brush in his mouth and daubs non-toxic paint onto the canvas. He even signs each artwork by stepping onto the canvas wearing a painted horseshoe.

HISS-TERICAL A snake spent six months in a wall cavity behind the toilet in a woman's apartment in Allschwil, Switzerland. After escaping from the flat above, the 27-in-long (70-cm) corn snake slithered down into Anika Bauer's home where it hid until she discovered it on a trip to the bathroom.

FOX THIEF Anna Clark, of Sussex, England, was horrified when a fox brazenly ran off with her handbag in a car park—and amazed when a few minutes later the animal suddenly reappeared and dropped the bag meekly at her feet.

CAT CALL While James Cocksedge was out at work, his inquisitive pedigree Singapura kitten, Bruce, pawed at telephone buttons and called 999, the number for the U.K. emergency services. Tracing the silent call, police officers rushed round to the London flat and smashed down the front door, leaving Bruce's owner with a bill for several hundred pounds.

ORANGE CROC

Snappy, an 8-ft-long (2.4-m) saltwater crocodile that lives in captivity in Geelong, Australia, suddenly turned orange. He chewed water pipes in his tank, damaging the filter, which caused pH levels in the water to rise and red algae to form. The combination of the two prompted his startling change in color. He is expected to return to a more crocodilian green over time. Tracey Sandstrom, Snappy's keeper, said, "There's no change in his behavior, his aggression, or his territorialism. He's still a really nasty crocodile."

Tiny Puppy

Believe It or Not, these Viszla puppies, born in Xuzhou, China, are siblings of the same age. Dwarfed by its normal-sized brother, after 18 days the smaller puppy was still barely more than an inch (2.5 cm) long, and weighed under half an ounce (14 g).

A HELPING PAW Sandie, a Sheltie-collie and Staffordshire bull terrier cross, has performed countless jobs for her disabled owner Sue Line of Coventry, England, including doing the shopping, the laundry, and paying for the groceries. On trips to the store, Sandie puts the shopping in a bag, which she carries in her mouth, and at the checkout she can take money from Sue's purse and hand it to the sales clerk. Sandie loads the washing machine, separating the dirty clothes into light and dark piles, and locks the machine door before the cycle begins. She has also learned how to unlock the kitchen door to let herself out to the toilet—and always remembers to close it behind her on her way back.

PRIZE PIGLET A court in Primorye, Russia, seized a woman's piglet in October 2010 to pay her overdue debt after it was judged that the animal was her most valuable possession.

SHOW-JUMPING COW Regina Mayer from Laufen, Germany, has trained a cow on the family farm to jump fences like a horse. Denied a horse by her parents, teen Regina fulfilled her riding ambitions by spending hours training Luna the cow to get accustomed to having a rider on her back and to wearing a halter and saddle. Luna now understands commands such as "go," "stand," and "gallop."

NOSE FOR WINE With a nose that is 2,000 times more sensitive than a human's, bloodhound Louisa Bella has been trained as a wine tester by her owners, wine label proprietors Michelle Edwards and Daniel Fischl of Melbourne, Australia. After just two weeks of training, she could sniff out a tainted wine cork within 30 seconds.

TERRIER TERROR Sucked up by a twister that raged through Birmingham, Alabama, in April 2011, Mason, a terrier mongrel, managed to crawl back to his owners' home three weeks later despite suffering two broken front legs.

CANINE COUPLE Louise Harris of Essex, England, spent more than £20,000 on an elaborate wedding ceremony, complete with outdoor marquee, for her Yorkshire terrier Lola, and Mugly, a Chinese crested dog. On her special day, Lola wore a £1,000 wedding dress customized with 1,800 Swarovski crystals. Her outfit was adorned with a £400 pearl necklace, £250 Swarovski crystal leg cuffs, and a £350 Swarovski crystal leash. The groom looked resplendent in a tuxedo before the happy couple and their canine guests wolfed down a buffet of dog-friendly cupcakes.

WILD WOOD WEB

In 2010, spiders in Pakistan's Sindh province were forced from the ground by floodwaters. The arachnids took shelter in thousands of trees and stayed for months because the water did not recede. Eventually their new homes became entirely cocooned in thick webs, which according to locals helped control the number of malaria-carrying mosquitoes in the stagnant waters.

BEAR NECESSITY Scientists working north of Alaska tracked a polar bear that swam for nine days straight, 426 mi (687 km) across the Beaufort Sea to an ice floe. That's the equivalent to the distance between Washington, D.C., and Boston, Massachusetts. Polar bears have been forced to swim longer distances to reach land in areas where the sea ice is shrinking.

Daisy the dog

TOWER

JUL 29 NITTY GRITTY BAND
OCT 12 CHINESE ACROBATS
OCT 27 MILES DAVIS TRIBUTE

TOWER
TOWER MEMBERS
TAKE 20% OFF
2011–2012 SERIES

YOUR UPLOADS

www.ripleys.com/submit

Is it a bird? Is it a plane? No, it's the spectacular flying Chihuahua. Photographer James Holmdahl of Bend, Oregon, attaches his 5-lb (2.3-kg) dog named Daisy to a cluster of helium balloons and sees her soar into the skies at a Fourth of July Parade.

R **LONG JOURNEY** Four months after disappearing from her home in Cornwall, England, a collie named Lucy mysteriously turned up 500 mi (800 km) away in a garden in Edinburgh, Scotland. Her owners, Sonya and Billy McKerron, made a 20-hour round trip to collect her.

R **SNIFFER HOGS** Believe it or not, wild hogs can detect smells up to 7 mi (11 km) away and 25 ft (7.6 m) underground.

R **MISSING MATE** Pei Pei, a male orangutan at China's Yunnan Wild Animal Park, was so distraught when his mate La Tewhen was moved to an adjoining enclosure while she was pregnant that he started digging a tunnel in the hope of being reunited with her.

R **POOP FOR GOLD** Dog owners in New Taipei City, Taiwan, were given the chance to turn their pets' poop into gold. In an attempt to clean up the streets, anyone handing in a bag of dog poop was entered in a lucky draw, the top prize for which was $2,100 in gold bars.

R **SEA DOG** Just Nuisance, a Great Dane from Simon's Town, South Africa, was inducted into the British Royal Navy in 1939. He never went to sea, but as an official Able Seaman he performed a number of promotional duties ashore and was once taken up in a plane to look for submarines. He was buried with full military honors in 1944 and a statue was erected in his memory. Since 2000, there has been an annual parade of Great Danes in Simon's Town from which the best look-alike is chosen.

R **JAWS BEACH** In September 2010, a fisherman caught a tiger shark off Jaws Beach in the Bahamas and a human left leg fell from its mouth. When the shark's belly was slit open, police found a right leg, two arms, and a torso, and were able to use fingerprints to identify the victim as a missing sailor. The beach was used as the location for the 1987 shark movie *Jaws: The Revenge*.

▣ POP STAR Anastasia, a Jack Russell terrier owned by Doree Sitterly of southern California, can pop 100 balloons in 44.49 seconds—that's faster than two balloons per second.

▣ CANINE MAYOR Lucy Lou, a border collie, was elected mayor of Rabbit Hash, Kentucky, in 2008, defeating rival political candidates that included a cat, a jackass, an opossum, and several other dogs.

Dogs in Disguise

These canine competitors were participants in a creative dog-grooming competition in Pasadena, California. Creative grooming events are hugely popular in the U.S. Owners trim their poodles to resemble zebras, lions, ponies, snails, and American footballers or movie characters such as Captain Jack Sparrow from *Pirates of the Caribbean.*

▣ TINY POLICE DOG A long-haired Chihuahua has been accepted as a police dog in Japan's Nara prefecture. Momo, who weighs just 6 lb 10 oz (3 kg), passed a search-and-rescue test by finding a person in five minutes after merely sniffing their cap. Momo specializes in rescue operations following disasters such as earthquakes, where she can squeeze her tiny body into places too small for normal rescue dogs.

▣ WIFE ATTACKS TIGER A man who was attacked by a tiger while hunting squirrels near his home in Malaysia was saved when his 55-year-old wife began hitting the big cat over the head with a wooden soup ladle. Han Besau ran to the rescue of Tambun Gediu after hearing his screams and instinctively beat the tiger with the ladle, causing it to flee.

▣ TORTOISE WHEEL A tortoise that lost a front leg after it was severed by a rat while she was hibernating can now outrace other tortoises thanks to a toy tractor wheel being fitted in place of the missing limb. Philip Chubb of Norwich, England, made a brace out of metal and velcro strips to fasten the wheel to the shell of Tuly the tortoise.

■▬ A TWO-HEADED CALF WAS BORN IN JANUARY 2011 IN MARTVILI, GEORGIA, THAT COULD EAT WITH BOTH ITS HEADS! ▬■

▣ BLOOD POPSICLES To keep its tigers cool during the scorching April of 2011, London Zoo gave them special popsicles made with blood.

▣ EEL POWER Finland's Helsinki Sea Life Center found an environmentally friendly way of powering its Christmas lights—by using an electric eel. Four plastic-encased steel probes were built to capture the eel's 650-volt discharge and filter it through to the lights, which shone particularly brightly at the eel's feeding time.

▣ NO CONTEST In 2010, a 150-lb (68-kg) mountain lion was chased up a tree in South Dakota by Chad Strenge's Jack Russell terrier, Jack, who weighed just 17 lb (7.7 kg).

▣ THICK FUR The furry chinchillas of South America have fur so dense that 50 hairs grow out of a single hair follicle.

SWIMMING WITH BEARS

Appearances can be deceiving. Children at the Cochrane Polar Bear Habitat in Ontario, Canada, look to be swimming right next to the most feared predators on Earth, but what you can't see is a 10-in-thick (25-cm) plexiglass barrier that separates the humans from the bears, allowing the children to swim in safety.

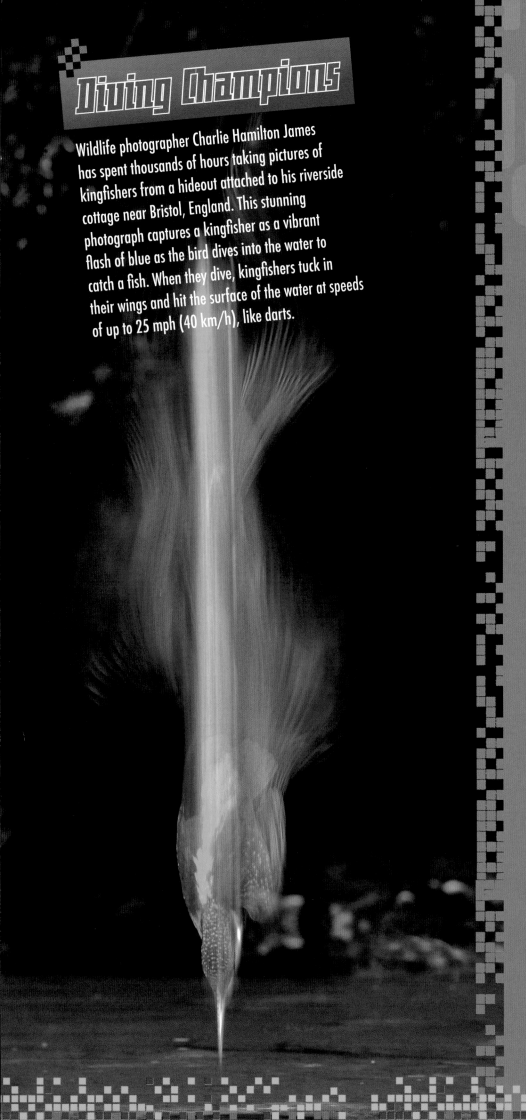

Diving Champions

Wildlife photographer Charlie Hamilton James has spent thousands of hours taking pictures of kingfishers from a hideout attached to his riverside cottage near Bristol, England. This stunning photograph captures a kingfisher as a vibrant flash of blue as the bird dives into the water to catch a fish. When they dive, kingfishers tuck in their wings and hit the surface of the water at speeds of up to 25 mph (40 km/h), like darts.

TIGHT SPOT A black bear was released back into a forest near Newport, Tennessee, after spending at least three weeks with a plastic jar stuck on its head. Before being removed by state wildlife officers, the jar had hindered the bear's attempts to feed, as a result of which the animal weighed only 115 lb (52 kg), barely half its healthy weight.

GOLD FISH Curt Carish of Kaua'i, Hawaii, caught a fish that had swallowed a gold watch—and the watch was still ticking and keeping correct time.

BIG BIRD The Newby family from Essex, England, share their home with a 6-ft-tall (1.8-m) pet emu named Beaky. The 196-lb (89-kg) bird was hatched from an egg by dad Iain, who works at an animal rescue center, and Beaky has become so much part of the family that she watches TV with them. She eats 14 lb (6.4 kg) of corn a week, 5 lb (2.3 kg) of fruit and vegetables, plus anything else she can find, including keys, sponges, and drill bits.

NEW MOM A wild lynx kitten that had been abandoned by its mother was adopted by a spaniel at a wildlife park in Kadzidlowo, Poland. Kraska the spaniel, who had just given birth to a litter of puppies, readily accepted six-month-old Mis the lynx as one of her own.

GOOSE PATROL A Canada goose and her goslings were given a police escort on a Washington State highway in June 2011. Three police cars closed two lanes of traffic on the busy Seattle highway during morning rush hour while they guided the geese to the nearest exit.

UNDERWEAR THIEF Benji the pet kangaroo escaped from his owner's home in Prague, Czech Republic, and hopped through neighboring gardens collecting women's underwear from washing lines as he did so. He was caught after one victim saw him escaping with her panties.

HOSTILE HOME The most heavily armed border zone in the world—between North and South Korea—has become a refuge for the red-crowned crane, one of the rarest birds on the planet. This is because it is such a restricted area that there is very little human activity to disturb the birds.

Monkey Business

For Connie Tibbs, her five pet macaque monkeys are part of the family. They play on the trampoline in the back garden of the family home in Pekin, Illinois, join her three children in the swimming pool, and even go horseback riding. One monkey is so skilled that it can ride a horse unaided. Connie also takes one of the monkeys—dressed in pajamas—to bed every night, much to the amusement of her husband Steve.

Connie bathes the monkeys to keep them clean and then dresses one of them in pajamas and takes it to bed with her.

Connie with her much-loved pet macaque monkeys at her home in Illinois.

Connie is so devoted to her pet monkeys that she even takes them out shopping.

BELIEVE IT OR NOT, THE TEXAS HORNED LIZARD CRIES BLOOD

This feisty lizard really pushes the envelope when it comes to warding off attackers. It forces jets of blood from its own eyes when threatened by a predator. It's possible for humans to squirt liquid from their tear ducts, but this is one step further. It can squirt its own blood, which contains an unpleasant-tasting toxin, for more than 5 ft (1.5 m). These lizards are not alone in their disturbing defense mechanisms.

South African armored crickets can not only splash blood from their insect armpits, but also vomit. The Spanish ribbed newt, on the other hand, contorts its rib bones so that they break the animal's skin and become a row of sharp, poison-tipped weapons. Fortunately, stabbing itself multiple times through its own torso does not seem to have an adverse effect on the Spanish newt.

NOISY BUG Although just 0.08 in (2 mm) long, the lesser water boatman, a pond insect that swims upside down using two long legs as paddles, produces 99.2 decibels of noise—louder than any other animal relative to its body size, and the equivalent of listening to an orchestra playing at full volume from the front row.

WONDER WEB The newly discovered Darwin's bark spider of Madagascar builds webs that cover an area of 30 sq ft (2.8 sq m) and span gaps over 80 ft (25 m) across.

ARMY OF CLONES Every insect in a nest of *Mycocepurus smithii* ants from Latin America is a clone of the queen. The species reproduces asexually from a single parent and is entirely male-free, which removes the stress of finding a mate.

RAINBOW ANTS

Dr. Mohamed Babu of Mysore, India, set up this eye-catching experiment whereby ants turned different colors after drinking sugar drops mixed with edible red, green, blue, and yellow coloring. As the ant's abdomen is semi-transparent, they absorb the colors as they sip the liquid. His wife gave him the idea after showing him how ants turned white after drinking spilt milk.

DEATH MARCH Army ants that begin marching in a circle can end up marching endlessly by the thousands in the same circle until they all die from exhaustion or starvation.

MONSTER MOLARS In proportion to its body size, the deep-sea fangtooth fish has the largest teeth of any sea creature—its skull has special sockets to hold the teeth and allow it to close its mouth. The fish itself is only 6 in (15 cm) long, but its teeth can reach nearly ¾ in (2 cm) in length. If these proportions were replicated in a great white shark, it would have teeth 2 ft 6 in (76 cm) long.

STICKY PROBLEM An estimated 14 million bees got loose in July 2011 after a delivery truck carrying more than 400 hive boxes and honey overturned on a highway in Fremont County, Idaho. Trying to avoid being stung, crews worked throughout the day to remove all the honey from the road.

TRAIN CRASH On April 27, 2011, termites chewed through a tree branch that then fell onto train tracks, causing a crash in Taiwan that killed five people and injured around a hundred others.

BELLY FLOP New Zealand's Maud Island frogs don't croak, they don't have webbed feet, and when they hop they land on their belly instead of their feet.

LIGHT MEAL *Atolla wyvillei*, a deep-sea species of jellyfish, starts glowing brightly when being attacked by its prey in an attempt to attract other predators that will attack its assailant. Its glow is so bright it can be seen from 300 ft (90 m) away.

SPEED BUG The fastest species of tiger beetle can run at 5.6 mph (9 km/h), which, relative to its body length, is the equivalent of a human running at 480 mph (770 km/h)—about 17 times the speed of Usain Bolt. The beetles move so quickly that their eyes and brain are unable to process vision in sync with their movement and they momentarily go blind, needing to stop and start several times while in hot pursuit of prey.

MICE CROSSING A council in South Wales has spent £190,000 on building bridges for dormice. The three overhead walkways were put up so that the little rodents could cross a busy road safely.

14 in (35 cm) long

ACTUAL SIZE

◆ **Bat Killer**

The Amazonian giant centipede is so powerful and agile that it can catch and eat bats. An adult centipede reaches 14 in (35 cm) long—the length of a man's forearm—and is able to climb the walls of caves. BBC cameraman Tim Green spent two weeks in a cave in Venezuela waiting to film this unique event. Eventually, he witnessed this fearsome beast hang down from the cave ceiling, grab a passing bat with some of its 46 legs, and kill it with its venom. It then devoured every piece of bat flesh over the next hour.

RARE BABY

A farmer in Hebron, Palestine, feeds milk to a newborn goat with two heads. The extremely rare condition, in which animals are born with more than one head, is called polycephaly.

BIRD'S-EYE VIEW In a case of real life imitating art, Bobby Haas took a stunning aerial photograph of a colony of hundreds of flamingoes off the coast of the Yucatán Peninsula, Mexico, that had arranged themselves into the shape of a giant flamingo.

SCREAMING TADPOLES Scientists in Argentina have discovered tadpoles that can scream. The larvae of the Argentine horned frog, which are carnivorous and eat other species of tadpole, emit a short, audible "metallic-like" sound.

AGILE GOAT When Yang Yang the goat was born without hind legs in Liaoning Province, China, farmer Lu Shanlu trained the unfortunate animal to walk on its forelegs. Within three months, Yang Yang could run around his yard several times on two legs without stopping.

RODENT COUTURE In May 2011, New York City staged a fashion show with a difference—the models were all rats. The sociable rodents showed their loveable side, dressed in miniature tutus, wedding dresses, and other flattering outfits. Rats have become popular pets in recent years.

GUARD GOAT Zhao Huaiyun of Sichuan Province, China, has trained his pet goat to act as a guard dog. As well as warding off stray dogs from his owner's property, the goat makes sure Zhao answers his cell phone, if he hasn't heard it, by running up to him, putting its forelegs on his arms, and baaing nonstop.

HASTY HIPPOS With a top speed of around 25 mph (40 km/h), an adult hippo can outrun a person in a short sprint. Hippos keep fit by walking up to 6 mi (10 km) a night foraging for food.

NO EYES Rowan, a German Spitz dog owned by Sam Orchard of Bedfordshire, England, was born without eyes but is able to navigate its way around by echolocation, using its barks.

MONKEY BOUNTY In October 2010, Yuki Yoneyama of Mishima, Japan, claimed a 200,000-yen ($2,600) bounty for capturing a wild macaque monkey that had bitten more than 100 people.

TOXIC MUD The bearded goby fish of coastal Africa thrives in toxic mud, can live for hours without oxygen, and eats jellyfish.

FEATHERED FIEND Shanna Sexton of Devon, England, became so annoyed by what she thought was a faulty smoke alarm sounding nonstop for seven days that she called in workmen to try to locate the problem. Then she discovered the culprit was an African Gray Parrot named Sammi, who had escaped from a neighbor's house and spent the week hidden in Shanna's garden mimicking the beeping sound of an alarm.

RARE FLY The Terrible Hairy Fly is a flightless species of fly that breeds in bat feces and has only been found in a single Kenyan cave. A specimen collected in 2010 was the first to be tracked down since 1948.

COOL ROOSTERS To stop fights breaking out between roosters, farmers in Chengdu, China, clothed the birds in plastic sunglasses. The glasses made it difficult for them to see each other and so made them less aggressive.

ROLLING TOADS Venezuela's pebble toad flees predators by rolling like a ball down the rocky inclines of its mountainous home—without coming to any harm. Pebble toads breed communally, and a single nest has been found to contain 103 toads and 321 eggs.

Master of Disguise

The Satanic leaf-tailed gecko is a lizard with a devilish disguise that enables it to adjust its body color to blend in with its surroundings. With its coiled shape, its camouflage is so effective that it is barely visible against these dead leaves in a national park in Madagascar.

R BEAVERING AWAY Beavers within Wood Buffalo National Park in Alberta, Canada, have spent decades building and maintaining a massive dam that measures a staggering half a mile (800 m) long.

R BIG SCHOOL Schools of Atlantic herring can stretch for more than 25 mi (40 km) and number millions of individual fish.

R FIGHTING SPURS Several species of South American birds called screamers have spurs on their wings that they use for fighting. The spurs can break off in another bird's body, but will grow back.

R LIGHT SWARM A worker honeybee weighs about 1/300th of an ounce (90 mg), meaning that a swarm of 50,000 bees weighs only 10 lb (4.5 kg).

‹‹YOUR UPLOADS

www·ripleys·com/submit

Poultry breeder Diane Kolpin from Lake Placid, Florida, sent us this picture of a baby chicken without any eyes. The bird had no eye sockets at all—just skin and feathers where its eyes should be—yet, given loving care, it has grown into a healthy, if blind, bird.

TIGHT FIT

A bullock in Ayrshire, Scotland, was rescued by animal charity officers after getting its head stuck between the rungs of a ladder in its field in August 2011. The Belgian blue bull was returned to its herd unharmed after the unfortunate incident.

R **$1.5M PUPPY** A red Tibetan mastiff puppy named Hong Dong was sold for $1.5 million in 2011. Tibetan mastiffs are fierce guard dogs and are rarely found outside Tibet, which makes them highly exclusive and sought-after. Hong Dong was bred in Qingdao, China, and weighed more than 180 lb (82 kg) at 11 months.

R **TREE-EATING FISH** A newly discovered species of armored catfish in the Amazon chews on the wood of fallen trees. Whereas other types of catfish use their teeth to scrape organic matter from the surfaces of submerged wood, this species actually ingests wood. The wood is subsequently expelled as waste, passing through the fish's body in less than four hours.

R **HIPPO HYGIENE** At China's Shanghai Zoo, keepers use giant toothbrushes to clean the teeth of adult hippos. The hippos, whose mouths measure up to 4 ft (1.2 m) wide, are fed on fruit and vegetables, which would clog up their teeth if they weren't brushed three times a week.

R **HERO HUSKY** Nanook, a Siberian Husky cross, instinctively knew that her owner Coleen Kilby from St. Catharines, Ontario, was about to suffer a heart attack in the middle of the night. The dog started howling, barking, and licking her face, and on waking up, Coleen felt chest pains and was rushed to hospital. If the heart attack had occurred while she was asleep, it could have been fatal.

R **DOGGIE FACELIFTS** Grandmother Amanda Booth from Melbourne, Australia, is using her life savings to pay $15,000 a year on facelifts for Shar Pei dogs to prevent them from suffering eye problems. The designer dogs are bred to have folds of floppy flesh on their face, but the heavy skin forces their eyelids to turn in, causing their eyelashes to scratch their cornea, often leading to blindness.

R **PIRANHA TERROR** More than 15 people swimming off a popular tourist river beach in Cáceres, Brazil, lost toes and chunks of their legs and ankles in November 2011 after thousands of flesh-eating piranhas flooded the river. Piranhas are common in rivers on the outskirts of Cáceres, but this was the first time they had infiltrated the city itself.

R **DAY TRIP** Frankie, a six-year-old Jack Russell terrier, walked 2 mi (3.2 km) from his home in Gravesend, Kent, England, to the nearest train station and then boarded a train for a 30-minute journey to London. When he arrived in London, he was detained by station staff until his owners caught a train up from Kent to collect him.

R **WALKING UPRIGHT** Treasure, a one-year-old poodle, prefers to walk upright on his hind legs rather than on all four. His owner, Dou Xianhui of Jilin City, China, briefly trained Treasure to walk on two legs when he was a puppy—but now he walks like that for up to 30 minutes at a time.

FANCY FOOTWORK

This double-footed horse belonging to R. van Wert of Cincinnati, Ohio, was photographed in 1930. You wouldn't want that hoof standing on your foot!

Mutton Bustin'

Budding rodeo riders typically under the age of six and weighing no more than 60 lb (27 kg) try to hold on to a 180-lb (81-kg) ewe for six seconds in the sport of Mutton Bustin' that is sweeping the United States. To prevent injury, the young riders wear ice-hockey helmets, face guards, and protective vests.

Index

Page numbers in italic refer to the illustrations

Crazy Animals

ACKNOWLEDGMENTS

Front cover (t) James Holmdahl, (b) Scottish SPCA; **4** Katrina Bridgeford/Rex Features; **6–7** Steven Senne/AP/Press Association Images; **8** Katrina Bridgeford/Rex Features; **9** (t) Barcroft Media Ltd, (l) Bay Ismoyo/AFP/Getty Images, (r) John Little/Bizarre Archive.com, (c) Andi Fitriono/Demotix; **10** (t) Quirky China News/Rex Features; **10–11** (b) Reuters; **11** (r) Newspix/Rex Features, (c) ABC TV, (l) Panda Photo/FLPA; **12** Time & Life Pictures/Getty Images; **13** Sunshine Serpents/Rex Features; **14** (l, r) KeystoneUSA-ZUMA/Rex Features, (b) www.sell-my-photo.co.uk; **15** Andrew Forsyth/Solent News/Rex Features; **16** SWNS.com; **17** Ian Butler/Solent News/Rex Features; **18** (t) © Photoshot, (b) AP/Press Association Images; **19** WENN.com; **20** Jennifer Showalter; **21** Alex Coppel/Newspix/Rex Features; **22** (t) © UPPA/Photoshot, (b) Reuters; **23** James Holmdahl; **24** Ren Netherland/Barcroft Media; **25** Caters News; **26** Charlie Hamilton James/naturepl.com; **27** Laurentiu Garofeanu/Barcroft USA; **28** Mohamed Babu/Solent News/Rex Features; **29** Tim Green; **30** UPPA/Photoshot; **31** (t) © Thomas Marent/ardea.com, (b) Diane Kolpin; **32** (t) Scottish SPCA, (b/l) Wool Warriors/Barcroft USA, (b/r) Mary Schwalm/AP/Press Association Images; **33** (b) The Canadian Press/Press Association Images; Back cover Andrew Cunningham, Cummings School of Veterinary Medicine, Tufts University

Key: t = top, b = bottom, c = center, l = left, r = right, sp = single page, dp = double page

All other photos are from Ripley Entertainment Inc.
Every attempt has been made to acknowledge correctly and contact copyright holders and we apologize in advance
for any unintentional errors or omissions, which will be corrected in future editions.